Puppy Show

by Sallie Carson

Illustrated by Karol Kaminski

Glenview, Illinois • Boston, Massachusetts • Chandler, Arizona
Upper Saddle River, New Jersey

puppies

Abby and Caleb giggled as the puppies jumped around them. Mom looked serious.

"Raising puppies is a big job," she said. "Puppies need food and water. They need to take walks every day. Most of all, they need to learn to behave."

behave: act correctly

Caleb picked up his <mark>wiggling</mark> puppy. "Don't worry," Caleb said. "Puppy training is our <mark>4-H</mark> project. We can start tomorrow."

"Yes," said Abby. "When the puppies are six months old, they can enter the 4H puppy show. My puppy will win!"

---

wiggling: moving and twisting back and forth
4-H: a club for boys and girls

The next day, the children put leashes on the puppies. When the puppies tried to run away, Caleb and Abby called "Come!" and pulled on their leashes.

As soon as the puppies learned one command, the children taught them a new one.

Extend Language **Now and Before**

Some actions happened in the past, and some happen now. Action words help you understand when things happen.

Now	Past
pull	pulled
learn	learned
wag	wagged
stay	stayed
call	called

Caleb and Abby practiced with the puppies for a short time every day. The puppies were **a real handful**. The first thing they learned was the word *no*.

tail

After training the puppies, Caleb and Abby played with them. The puppies wagged their tails.

That was a good thing. Mom told the children, "**Before you know it**, it will be time for the 4-H puppy show!"

Extend Language **Idioms**

a real handful: something hard to control

before you know it: very soon

On the day of the show, the
4-H club members walked their puppies
around the ring. The puppies had learned
all their commands. They heeled, sat,
stayed, and came when they were called.

Every puppy won a prize! Abby was
right. Her puppy *did* win.